SOMERSET CRICKET

SOMERSET CRICKET
The Glory Years
1973-1987

Alain Lockyer
with text by Richard Walsh

HALSGROVE

First published in Great Britain in 2012

ISBN 978 0 85704 113 5

HALSGROVE
Halsgrove House,
Ryelands Business Park,
Bagley Road, Wellington, Somerset TA21 9PZ
Tel: 01823 653777   Fax: 01823 216796
email: sales@halsgrove.com

Part of the Halsgrove group of companies.
Information on all Halsgrove titles is available at: www.halsgrove.com

Printed in China by Everbest Printing Co Ltd

Contents

Foreword
by Roy Kerslake

"The Glory Years!" Probably the three most evocative words in the history of Somerset County Cricket Club. Founded in 1875, it is a history rich in so many ways, and yet lacking, in the main, one vital ingredient…silverware!

That all changed in a short, golden era that ran from 1979 to 1983, when Somerset reigned supreme as the kings of domestic one-day cricket, and during which, after 104 years of unrewarded effort, five trophies returned to the County Ground in Taunton.

As Chairman of the Club's Cricket Committee at that time, I was privileged to have been able to experience those triumphs at close quarters. For me, the origins of our success can be traced back to the arrival in 1971 of that most redoubtable of Yorkshiremen, Brian Close, who brought to the dressing-room a mix of skill, grit and northern wit in equal measure.

Along with older pros like Tom Cartwright, Mervyn Kitchen and Graham Burgess, Close (as captain from 1972) nurtured an emerging crop of talented youngsters – including a couple of likely lads called Botham and Richards – and instilled in them an inner-belief and winning mentality that was to have a profound effect on the Club's fortunes at the turn of the decade.

By that stage, Brian Rose was now at the helm (and, in 1978, it is worth noting he was the youngest County captain in the country). And it is to "Rosey's" enormous credit that he possessed the ability to mould a side containing both artists and artisans into a unit willing and able to run through a brickwall for each other.

Indeed, looking back, the sense of pride at what those players achieved is only matched by a sense of wonder at how the team came together at the right time and at the right place. For, within its ranks was one of the greatest two or three batsmen ever to play the game (Vivian Richards), ditto in terms of the world's best all-rounder (Ian Botham), as well as, arguably, the finest one-day bowler of all time (Joel Garner).

And this 'holy trinity' was joined by a truly outstanding group of local talent, which included Peter Denning, Peter Roebuck, Vic Marks, Phil Slocombe, Keith Jennings and Colin Dredge. Call it good planning, call it serendipity, call it what you will! Whatever it might have been, it was unmistakably an incredible time to be a Somerset supporter.

Of course, Somerset being Somerset, we had to experience the depths of despair before finally enjoying a first taste of victory, and, perhaps, because of that it tasted all the sweeter. Thus, the agony of the first weekend in September 1978 had to be endured before the ecstasy of the 8 and 9 September 1979 could be treasured. The symmetry of the respective climaxes to the '78 and '79 seasons is remarkable to behold, as is their ultimately contrasting endings.

Consequently, just as I can recall the names of England's World Cup winning side of '66, so my son, Jon (who was 10 at the time), can still reel-off the list (in batting order) of his heroes who won the Gillette Cup at Lord's for Somerset in '79: Rose, Denning, Richards, Roebuck, Botham, Marks, Burgess, Breakwell, Garner, Taylor and Jennings.

Sadly, not all of those players are still with us, but I hope this book will bear fitting witness to their legacy.

I hope, too, that the Club's current crop of exciting young cricketers may draw some inspiration from the deeds of their predecessors. If the last few seasons, from a Somerset perspective, can be dubbed "The Nearly Years," let's hope that "The Glory Years – Part 2" is a book still waiting to be written!

In the meantime, I hope that the collection of some of Alain Lockyer's evocative photos contained inside the pages of this book will help you to relive those heady days of 30 odd years ago.

Roy Kerslake (President Somerset CCC)

Introduction
by Alain Lockyer

Taking photographs is something that provides enjoyment to most people, so to take photographs and make a living from it is even better.

Capturing the images that appear in this book was very much a labour of love – it was work as well as providing me with a huge amount enjoyment.

To be involved with the Somerset players in the way that I was as well as being part of the events that took place during the Glory Years became a great source of pleasure.

My interest in taking photographs first came from my father who was a photographer during the Second World War. He gave me his cameras and it went on from there and while I was at school in Taunton this interest was encouraged and developed further.

I started taking photographs professionally on a part time basis for the *Somerset County Gazette* in Taunton and received a lot of help from staff photographer Leslie Charrett.

When I set out as a full time press photographer in 1973 the equipment used was very different to what we use today. I used to stand on the boundary edge with a Rolliflex, a twin lens reflex camera, with no telephoto lens, hoping that a fielder would come near to where I was standing.

However with the coming of 35mm cameras and Novaflex sports lens taking pictures took a big step forward. Most of the photographs included in this book were taken with this type of equipment.

At about this time I joined as a photographic partner of Somerset News and our involvement with the Club increased.

We had one of the last wire machines in the country and had to develop our own pictures, which we sometimes did in the washroom that was situated at the back of what is now the Old Pavilion. After that we often dried them with a hairdryer!

These pictures were then supplied to the national and international press, including the *Sun* who gave me my break in Fleet Street, *The Times* and *Sunday Times*, the *Guardian* and the *Daily Express* series.

Over the years I developed a good rapport with the Somerset players, which enabled me to gain a real insight into their lives as professional sportsmen resulting in the pictures that are inside these covers.

The picture that sticks in my memory from that time is the one I took of Ian Botham, Joel Garner and Viv Richards on the day of their final match for Somerset. The Big Three sent a messenger out to me on the field, where there were as many as 50 other photographers waiting for a glimpse of them, and they posed for that picture, which they said was my going away present and that still means so much to me.

Finally I would like to put on record my appreciation for my co author Richard Walsh who was responsible for writing and collating the captions and text for this stroll down Memory Lane.

We hope you derive as much pleasure from the book as we did putting it together.

Alain Lockyer

The Alain Lockyer Glory Years Archive

An introduction by Richard Walsh

Mention the Glory Years to any Somerset supporter and whatever their age they will know exactly what you are talking about – that period in the Club's history during which they won their first ever silverware since being formed in 1875.

The five years referred to by the Glory Years are those between 1979 and 1983, when Brian Rose captained the side to success in five one-day competitions.

However it was under the stewardship of Brian Close, who preceded Rose as skipper between 1972 and 1977, that the trophy winning Somerset team was developed.

It was Close who nurtured a number of highly talented young players, many local, including all rounder Ian Botham, brought up and educated in Yeovil, along with Viv Richards, brought over from the West Indies after being spotted by Len Creed, the Somerset Chairman.

At the same time as Botham and Richards were arriving at the County Ground, Alain Lockyer, a young Taunton-based press photographer started to ply his trade.

This book contains a selection of his pictures, mostly from the period 1973-1987, chosen by and captioned by Alain himself to illustrate the Glory Years and the essential years which framed them, a collection now under the ownership of the Somerset Cricket Museum.

Living in Taunton and being a regular visitor to the County Ground the local photographer built up a strong link with all of the players during that period, something which is witnessed by the fact that they allowed him to photograph them both on and off the field.

When Close arrived at Taunton in 1971 after a long and illustrious career with Yorkshire he was already 40 years old. He played one season under the leadership of Brian Langford before taking over the captaincy in 1972.

The vastly experienced Close, supported by a handful of senior professionals, turned out to be exactly the right person to develop the crop of youngsters emerging through the Somerset ranks.

In his first season as skipper Close inherited a mixture of youth and experience in the side, including long serving Somerset players batsmen Merv Kitchen from Nailsea and Taunton-born Roy Virgin, off spinner Brian Langford, who although born in Birmingham grew up in the county, Tom Cartwright, who had a long career with Warwickshire before moving to the south west, wicket-keeper Derek Taylor from Surrey and former Sussex strike bowler Allan Jones. All rounder Peter Robinson who joined Somerset from Worcestershire in 1965 was also in the team.

Three more local players, all rounder Graham Burgess from Glastonbury and two blonde-haired batsmen Brian Rose, who spent all but the first three weeks of his life in Weston-super-Mare, and Peter Denning from Chewton Mendip, who both made their debuts for the county in 1969 were already in the side.

Barbadian-born quick bowler Hallam Moseley joined Somerset in 1971 while the club also recruited Australian wrist spinner Kerry O'Keefe to join the ranks that year.

1973 saw the arrival of 25 year old left arm spinner Dennis Breakwell, from Northamptonshire, who was also a more than useful batsman, along with the vastly experienced 41 year old wicket-keeper batsman Jim Parks from Sussex, while Bob Clapp a tall fast bowler from Weston-super-Mare also made his debut.

Between 1971 and 1973 Somerset enjoyed relative success and achieved mid table positions in both the Championship and John Player League, which was then a Sunday afternoon competition.

However things were going to change as a result of a committee decision to pursue a youth policy, which was proposed by Roy Kerslake who at the time was Chairman of Cricket.

The start of the 1974 season saw the arrival of Botham, batsmen Peter Roebuck from Millfield School, Phil Slocombe from Weston-super-Mare and Millfield, and Richards along with another all rounder Vic Marks who hailed from the South Somerset village of Middle Chinnock and had attended Blundell's School at Tiverton.

Botham first came to the cricketing world's attention in the Benson and Hedges quarter final that year at the County Ground, when in reply to Hampshire's 182, the hosts had slumped to 113 for eight, hardly a winning position. Botham had other ideas and despite being hit in the mouth by West Indian paceman Andy Roberts he went on to score an unbeaten 45 to see Somerset to an unlikely victory.

That season saw the county reach the semi finals in both the Benson and Hedges and the Gillette Cup competitions and second place in the John Player League – their best ever since the advent of one day cricket.

Another local lad Keith Jennings from Milverton, whose bowling and close fielding was to become invaluable, first appeared on the Somerset scene in 1975. However after all of the excitement of the previous season, the results were disappointing.

Colin Dredge a fast bowler from Frome arrived in 1976, when Somerset were strong contenders for the John Player League.

Going into the last round of matches only needing to beat 16th placed Glamorgan at Cardiff to lift the title, they failed to win by one run, and had to settle for joint second place, in spite of playing the whole season without Richards who was with the West Indian tourists in England.

Close signed off his period of captaincy in style in 1977 by leading a Somerset side, that included debutant opening bowler Joel Garner, a West Indian playing Lancashire League Cricket for Littleborough, to victory over Australia by seven wickets at Bath.

The Gillette Cup proved to be Somerset's most successful one day competition in 1977, but after reaching the semi final they lost out to Middlesex at Lord's. In a match that was scheduled to take place on 17 August because of rain a 15 over game was eventually played on 26 August with Somerset losing by six wickets.

The departure of Close saw the appointment of 27 year old Rose to the captaincy for the 1978 season a job he embraced wholeheartedly and he proved to be an immediate success.

After leading the Championship in June, Somerset eventually ended up in fifth place, but it was once again in the one day competitions that the team enjoyed most success.

Somerset reached the semi-final of the 50 over Benson and Hedges competition, before losing out to Kent at Taunton in a rain interrupted game that took three days to complete.

However they were in contention in both the Gillette Cup and the John Player League until the final weekend of the season.

In the Gillette Cup they beat Warwickshire at home in the first round, Richards scoring an unbeaten 139 as they chased down a target of 292.

The second round saw Rose's team travel to Cardiff to face Glamorgan, where they won with 'Dasher' Denning hitting a magnificent 145.

Next opponents were Kent at Canterbury where Dredge claimed four for 23 to help his beloved county to victory and a home tie in the semi-final against Essex, and quite a game that turned out to be.

In front of a packed house at the County Ground the hosts opted to bat first and posted 287 for six, Richards making 116 and Roebuck 57. Essex in reply were all out for 287 off the last ball of the innings meaning that Somerset had won by losing fewer wickets and were on the way to Lord's and their first one day final appearance since 1967, when they lost to Kent.

Meanwhile in the John Player League, the team had won nine games in a row and were top of the table going into the last game of the season, which was to be played the Sunday after the Gillette Cup Final at Lord's.

Sadly for Somerset it was a weekend of double disappointment, losing out to Sussex at cricket's headquarters on Saturday, before returning home to face Essex which they also narrowly lost and eventually had to settle for being runners-up.

After coming so close for several years, 1979 saw Somerset break their duck in domestic competitions.

In the Gillette Cup, they comfortably accounted for Derbyshire at Taunton before beating Kent in the quarter final in dramatic fashion in front of another packed County Ground, when in reply to the hosts' 190, the visitors were bowled out for 60, Garner ending with five for 11 and Botham three for 15.

The semi-final saw a trip to Lord's to face Middlesex, where they triumphed by seven wickets, thanks to Garner who ended with four for 24 and Burgess who took three for 25 from his 12 overs, while in their reply Denning hit an unbeaten 90.

In the final Somerset faced Northamptonshire who won the toss and put Rose's team into bat.

Somerset scored 269 for eight from their 60 overs. The captain set the tone with 41 but it was Richards with an impressive 117, helped later by 27 from Botham and a tail end 24 from Garner that helped post what proved to be a winning total.

Northants in reply were bowled out for 224, Garner taking six for 29, to give Somerset victory by 45 runs!

However there was little chance to celebrate the success because the following day they had to play against Nottinghamshire at Trent Bridge in the final round of matches in the John Player League.

The situation at the top of the table before the game was such that if Somerset beat Nottinghamshire and other results went their way, they could win the John Player League title – which is exactly how things worked out.

After being put into bat for the second day in a row, Somerset made 185 for eight, Roebuck top scoring with 50 and Botham making 30, in reply to which Notts were bowled out for 129, Garner taking three for 16.

The 104 year wait for silverware was over and in the space of two days Somerset had lifted two trophies. This was the county's finest hour, not one but two cups in the space of 24 hours! Their time had come at last and Somerset were on the march, this was just the start of things to come.

Over the following four seasons under the captaincy of Rose the county proceeded to win three more one day trophies.

The next silverware for the County Ground trophy cabinet was the Benson and Hedges Cup in 1981, by which time Burgess had retired and been replaced by another very talented all rounder Nigel Popplewell.

In the semi-final Kent were defeated at Taunton, to earn Somerset a place in another Lord's final, against Surrey, who struggled against Garner (five for 14 off 11 overs) to reach 195 for eight off their allocated 55 overs.

Somerset replied with 197 for three, a total fashioned around Richards' unbeaten 132, an innings that won him the Man of the Match award.

Rose's team were also in contention for the Championship until the last round of matches, but in the end had to be content with third spot behind winners Nottinghamshire and Surrey.

After a slightly uneasy start to their Benson and Hedges campaign in 1982 Somerset eventually won their way through to the Lord's final where this time they faced Nottinghamshire.

Batting first the opposition were bowled out for 130 in 50.1 overs, Garner taking three for 13 off his 8.1 overs, while Botham, Marks and Dredge both picked up two wickets each.

Somerset made light work of the run chase and after losing Denning with the total on 27, Roebuck (53 not out) and Richards (51 not out) saw their side home to a nine wicket victory.

Somerset's last Lord's one day final appearance during the Glory Years was in 1983, a year which saw Rose miss the second half of the season with a back injury, resulting in the captaincy being taken over by other members of the side, including Botham and Roebuck.

The team that season included two more local players, all rounder Jeremy Lloyds, from Curry Rivel and wicket-keeper Trevor Gard, who hailed from South Somerset and had been on the staff for a number of years, in place of the ever dependable Taylor who had retired.

After a close encounter with Middlesex at Lord's in the semi-final of the NatWest Trophy, in which both teams scored 222, Somerset went through to the final by losing fewer wickets.

Somerset returned to Lord's in early September where they beat Kent by 24 runs in the final. After posting 193 for nine off their 50 overs, which included 51 from Richards, Kent were bowled out for 169 thanks to tight bowling from Garner, who conceded just 15 runs from his nine overs as well as economic spells from Botham and Marks and two leg side stumpings by Gard.

In 1983 Somerset finished runners-up in the John Player League, for the sixth time; although they ended level on points at the top of the table it was Yorkshire who took the title because they won more away games.

After winning the NatWest and ending second in the John Player League the previous season, 1984 was rather a disappointment. This was the season that saw Martin Crowe playing for Somerset with considerable success as a replacement for Richards and in the championship they climbed from 10th to seventh.

However the team led by new captain Botham or, when he was on England duty, his second in command Marks, who topped 1000 runs for the first time as well as taking 86 wickets, only reached the quarter finals of the one day competitions and 13th in the John Player League.

That season saw Roebuck and Popplewell enjoying considerable success with the bat, while left arm bowler Mark Davis from Kilve claimed 66 first class wickets.

The end of the season saw the retirement of Denning, a true local hero, who made his first team debut back in 1969 since when he had been very much part of the Somerset scene.

The highlights of the 1985 season were achieved with the bat. Richards set a new individual batting record for Somerset of 322 against Warwickshire at the County Ground in early June, eclipsing the previous best of 310 scored by Harold Gimblett against Sussex at Eastbourne in 1948. Botham also scored several quickfire centuries and amassed a total of 80 sixes for the County, a new Somerset record.

Despite these impressive feats Somerset ended bottom of the championship table for the first time since 1969, reached the quarter finals of the NatWest, were knocked out at the zonal stages of the Benson and Hedges Cup and finished 10th in the John Player League.

The season of 1986, the first full year under Roebuck's captaincy will be remembered more for events off the field rather than the team's performances. Two young batsmen, local boy Richard Harden and Nigel Felton both passed 1000 championship runs in a season for the first time, but overall the playing results were disappointing.

Somerset lifted themselves one place off the bottom of the championship table, in the NatWest they lost in the second round, they didn't progress beyond the zonal stages of the Benson and Hedges, but they did climb to sixth in the John Player League.

Towards the end of the season it was announced that Somerset would not be renewing the contracts of Garner and Richards and that they had signed Crowe on a three year deal as their overseas player, a decision that also led to the departure of Botham.

Despite the public outcry that ensued from many supporters The Big Three, who had each played a significant part in the Glory Years were to depart from the club at the end of the 1986 season and bring the curtain down on the most successful trophy winning period yet in the history of Somerset CCC.

However that wasn't the end of the matter and a special general meeting was called to take place at the Bath and West Showground on Saturday 8 November to discuss a motion of no confidence that had been passed in the committee by a members petition.

Members travelled to Shepton Mallet from far and wide and special coaches were laid on by the County to enable as many as possible to be present.

At the end of the meeting the motion of no confidence proposed by the those who opposed the committee's decision failed by 1828 votes to 798 and Botham, Garner and Richards departed from Somerset.

Botham went off to play for Worcestershire and Durham, while Richards ended his Championship career at Glamorgan.

For some feelings continued to run high, but eventually Botham, Garner and Richards each returned to the county where they had made their names in English cricket, to receive honorary life memberships.

Thankfully since then Botham has had a stand named in his honour, while Garner and Richards have both had entry gates to the County Ground dedicated to them.

Somerset CCC has moved on dramatically since that period and there have been numerous developments at the County Ground.

However at the time of writing Somerset has yet to match or improve upon the successes that they enjoyed in the Glory Years!

Sit back and enjoy Alain Lockyer's own selection of photographs from that era and see how many moments in time or faces in the crowd you can remember.

Somerset Players and Cricket

Ian Botham being presented with his first sponsored car, a Triumph TR7, by Taunton-based garage Wadham Stringer who were situated in East Street. Taunton, at the time.

This was one of the first pictures that I took of Ian Botham because we more or less started our involvement with Somerset at the same time. (Doesn't Ian look young!)

A picture of the Somerset squad in 1979. Don't they all look young!
Back row left to right: Trevor Gard, Keith Jennings, Hallam Moseley, David Gurr, Joel Garner, Colin Dredge, Peter Roebuck and Vic Marks. Front row left to right: Ian Botham, Viv Richards, Derek Taylor, Brian Rose, Peter Denning, Merv Kitchen and Dennis Breakwell.

Viv Richards taking to the pitch for Somerset during the Glory Years. Viv always placed his hand across his chest as a mannerism whenever he went out to field.

Peter Roebuck, who later went on to captain Somerset CCC is pictured enjoying the sunshine on the players' balcony of the Colin Atkinson Pavilion.

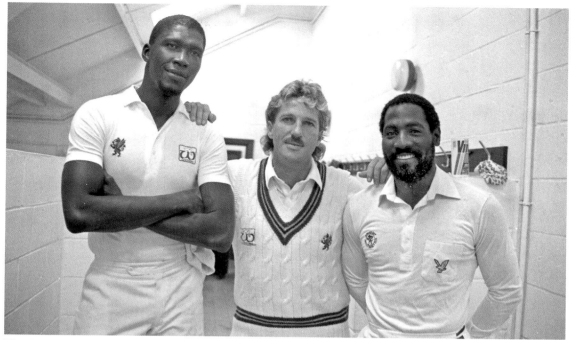

The Big Three – Joel Garner, Ian Botham and Viv Richards. This was a huge picture for me because it was their special leaving present before they departed from the club. The boys made a phone call and invited me to go upstairs into the dressing room where they posed for this picture together during their final game together for Somerset.

This is a unique picture and I am very proud of it because it marked the end of my involvement with the three of them collectively after a long period of time, a period that had given me a lot of fun and enjoyment.

Ian Botham arriving at the County Ground by helicopter for the first time, ahead of a one day game.

Viv Richards, on his arrival at the County Ground at the start of his Somerset career. This is one of the best pictures I ever took of 'The King!'

A young Viv Richards pictured with Greg Chappell who had enjoyed two very successful seasons with Somerset in 1968 and '69.

Viv Richards, going out to bat from the home dressing room to the side of the Old Pavilion. On the right are the steps down from the roof of the Ridley Stand that was demolished to make way for the creation of Gimblett's Hill.

Left of the picture is Len Jones, who was a well known figure at the County Ground and who latterly sold scorecards, while on the right is groundsman Don Price.

I used to spend a lot of time at the top of the Ridley Stand balcony steps which was a favourite camera position.

Ian Botham modelling Somerset's new shirt sponsored by Lyle and Scott. Vic Thrower who was the rep for Lyle and Scott was also an Olympic-standard champion at clay pigeon shooting.

Ian Botham resigns. Ian pictured in the committee room of the Colin Atkinson Pavilion after announcing his resignation in 1986. Also in the picture is Eric Coombes who was the cricket correspondent for the *Somerset County Gazette* at that time.

Ian Botham waves goodbye – his final innings for Somerset at the County Ground in 1986.

Ian Botham and Joel Garner walking down the steps of the Colin Atkinson Pavilion out onto the County Ground ahead of their final game for Somerset.

Viv Richards pictured with Darren Foster on the balcony at the County Ground. Richie Richardson played club cricket for Staplegrove locally before later going on to play for West Indies himself.

Brian Rose and Ian Botham taking the field at the County Ground, with Vic Marks in the background.

Vic Marks and Ian Botham going out to bat for Somerset at the County Ground.

Viv Richards – the King of the County Ground.

Little and Large! Joel Garner walks out ahead of wicket-keeper Trevor Gard.

Ian Botham enjoying the afternoon sunshine at Bath.

Ian Botham loses the jumper during a bowling spell at Taunton.

Ian Botham taking the field ahead of a charity football match at Chard Town FC – giving me my customary greeting. Vic Marks is one of the players in the background.

As well as his batting brilliance Viv Richards was a very useful off break bowler who captured 96 first class wickets as well as many victims in the one day games.

Ian Botham walking back to his bowling mark with a determined look.

Viv Richards in training ahead of the start of a new season. Ian Botham is in the background.

Vic Marks and Ian Botham enjoy a joke as they sit on the balcony of the Colin Atkinson Pavilion.

Peter Denning and Brian Rose make their way to the wicket together for the last time before Dasher retires.

Ian Botham at one of his early press calls at the County Ground.

Peter Denning walks out to open the batting for last time at the County Ground, followed by Brian Rose.

All the cameras are focussed on Ian Botham at an early press day photo shoot at the County Ground. Pictured third from the right is Stuart McDowell, from the *Sunday Independent* who was one of my early mentors. Look how many turned up for the press call on that occasion.

Nigel Popplewell looks worried after a stumping appeal.

Derek Taylor who joined Somerset from Surrey in 1970 and became an integral part of the team during the Glory Years before he retired in 1982. I used to enjoy taking pictures of Derek because he was one of the first 'keepers who threw himself around behind the stumps, resulting in good photographs.

A young Brian Rose who went on to lead Somerset to five one day trophies in as many seasons.

Brian Rose signs autographs after a Somerset success.

The Somerset squad in 1979. Back row left to right: Vic Marks, Peter Roebuck, Colin Dredge, Joel Garner, David Gurr, Hallam Moseley, Keith Jennings and Trevor Gard. Front row left to right: Dennis Breakwell, Merv Kitchen, Peter Denning, Brian Rose, Derek Taylor, Viv Richards and Ian Botham.

All rounder Peter Robinson, who joined Somerset from his native Worcestershire ahead of the 1965 season and went on to become County coach during the Glory Years and remained with the Club until he retired in 2008.

Dennis Breakwell (left), Vic Marks and Dasher Denning celebrate another memorable one day success.

Joel Garner and Viv Richards toast a Somerset victory with Desmond Haynes of Middlesex.

Somerset CCC squad pic in 1978, Brian Rose's first year as captain.

Back row left to right: Ian Botham, David Gurr, Colin Dredge, Peter Roebuck and Hallam Moseley. Middle row left to right: Phil Slocombe, Keith Jennings, Dennis Breakwell, Trevor Gard, Martin Olive and Peter Robinson. Front row left to right: Merv Kitchen, Peter Denning, Brian Rose, Derek Taylor and Graham Burgess.

Ian Botham stands in the field alongside young left-handed batsman Nigel Felton in front of the Executive Business Club which was next to the Stragglers Bar.

Hallam Moseley in action at Taunton.

Brian Close, Somerset captain from 1972-1977
leaves the field accompanied by a young admirer.
Keith Jennings is in the background.

An early picture of
Ian Botham, before a
batting session in the
nets at the County
Ground.

Viv Richards in action
– another effortless
shot from the
maestro.

Viv Richards and
Joel Garner inspecting
the wicket at the
County Ground
before the start of
a game.

Joel Garner and Viv Richards make their way out to field at the County Ground.

Viv Richards with Somerset coach Peter Robinson at pre-season nets.

A lap of honour for Viv Richards, training hard at the County Ground.

Joel Garner signing autographs during a benefit match at Milverton.

Indian star batsman Sunil Gavaskar spent the 1980 season with Somerset. He was a really nice man but didn't like the cold weather very much!

Joel Garner, the Big Bird in action in the NatWest Trophy.

A NatWest Trophy match in action at the County Ground. Joel Garner is walking back to his mark, Trevor Gard is the wicket-keeper, Colin Dredge is first slip, Ian Botham at second and Viv Richards in the gully.

More action from the same NatWest Trophy game. Joel Garner is the bowler and Sam Cook the umpire signalling a no-ball (top).

Wicket-keeper Trevor Gard and Ian Botham scatter the sawdust watched by Colin Dredge (right).

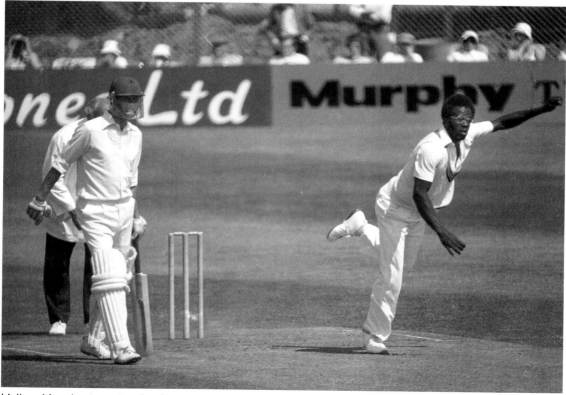

Hallam Moseley in action for Somerset.

'Big Bird' Joel Garner flying at Taunton.

Ace wicket keeper Trevor Guard in his other role as a Somerset batsman.

All rounder Nigel
Popplewell in bowling
action.

Derek Taylor keeping wicket at the County
Ground.

Colin Dredge, the Demon of Frome, in bowling action at the County Ground. The umpire is former Somerset player Ken Palmer.

Joel Garner is bowling, Derek Taylor is the keeper and Viv Richards is at first slip.

Ian Botham in bowling action. Ken Palmer is the umpire

Ian Botham is the close fielder and Derek Taylor the keeper as Dennis Breakwell tries to get a wicket for Somerset.

Richard Harden batting at Clarence Park, Weston-Super-Mare.

Ian Botham arriving for a
charity cricket match at
Yeovil.

A near miss for Viv
Richards.

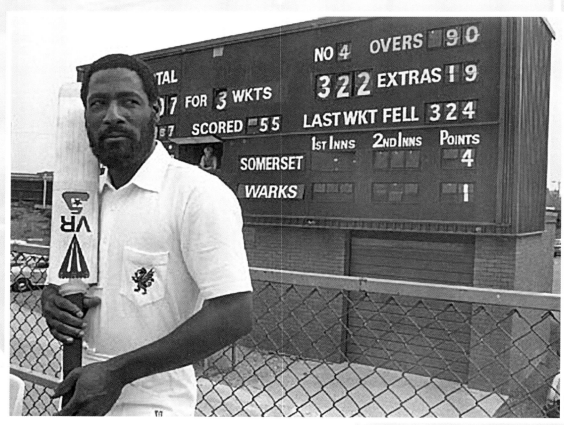

Viv Richards standing in front of the scoreboard after he had set a new Somerset record individual score of 322 against Warwickshire on 1 June 1985. Richards scored his runs in six minutes short of five hours, faced 258 balls and hit 42 fours and 8 sixes.

Viv Richards in defensive mode watching the ball carefully onto the bat.

Somerset Cricketers On and Off the Field

Colin Dredge, known to his friends as Herbie, was nicknamed the Demon of Frome by Alan Gibson. He was a big hearted bowler who was a very willing workhorse with the ball and key member of the team during the Glory Years.

New Zealander Martin Crowe pictured during his first stay with Somerset in 1984 when he joined the Club as a replacement for Viv Richards who was involved with the West Indies touring team to England that summer. Martin Crowe enjoyed a successful season and scored over 1800 runs, including six hundreds as well as taking 44 wickets.

Derek Taylor was the ever dependable gloveman who regularly stood up to Tom Cartwright. He started his career with Surrey, but with a name like Derek John Somerset Taylor he was surely always destined to play his part in the Glory Years team.

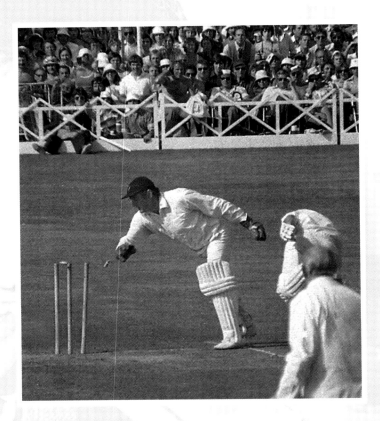

All rounder Vic Marks, known by all of his team-mates as 'the teacher' doing it for real at Taunton School. We had a lot of fun re-creating his 'teacher' nick-name, at Taunton School in his mortar board and gown.

Vic spent two terms teaching at Taunton School in the winter of 1985/6, having done something similar at Blundell's for three winters between 1978-80.

Kathy and Ian Botham and their first child Liam.

Proud parents Kathy and Ian Botham with their son Liam.

Ian Botham the big hitting batsman.

Ian Botham pictured at the boot of
his car at the County Ground
along with his personal assistant
Andy Withers.

Ian Botham warming
up ahead of his first
game back at County
Ground for
Worcestershire
against his former
county.

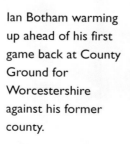

Ian Botham and Mike Brearley, two England captains pictured together at a Somerset match.

Brian Rose pictured in his Double Winners jumper in 1979.

Tony Brown, Secretary of SCCC pictured with Martin Crowe (right) and Tony Pigott who played at the time for Sussex CCC.

Although he was born in Cheshire, Ian Botham grew up in Yeovil and went to Milford Primary and Bucklers Mead School where he developed his talents as an all round sportsman.

He was a more than useful footballer and might have taken the game up professionally, but it was cricket that he chose. However he did sign to play for Yeovil Town FC before they gained league status and he is seen here completing the necessary registration forms with the Glovers player manager Gerry Gow.

Viv Richards, Brian Rose and Ian Botham celebrate another success with a glass of Dry Blackthorn Cider.

Ian Botham modelling a sheepskin jacket for Fenland Sheepskins.

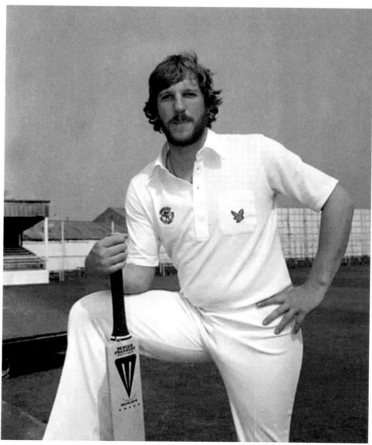

Ian Botham modelling Somerset's new Lyle and Scott cricket shirt.

Viv Richards collects his first sponsored car, a Ford Capri, from White Brothers in East Reach, Taunton. Jock McCombe, Viv's personal assistant is in the passenger seat.

Viv Richards with his first sponsored car at White Brothers in Taunton.

Viv Richards with Peter White, the Chairman of White Brothers, Taunton (right front) and the rest of the staff at the garage.

County Ground Scenes

Plenty of Test Match experience here – Basil D'Oliveira (left), Ian Botham and Mike Denness (right) offer a coaching session at the County Ground.

Somerset fans invade the pitch after another one day success.

All aboard! Preparing for the open top bus ride through Taunton in 1979 after winning the Gillette Cup and John Player League over the same weekend.

The players are all aboard and the bus is just about to leave the County Ground. Captain Brian Rose is standing up near the front of the bus, Dennis Breakwell is holding the John Player Trophy

aloft while just in front of him Ian Botham is enjoying a well deserved drink.

Dave Weadon and Norman Thompson, both press colleagues, along with myself had the pleasure of joining the players on the celebration bus ride through Taunton.

Ian Botham being interviewed by Westward TV on the roof of what was the Indoor School. The film cameraman is John Kingdon, while the soundman is Bob Woolmington.

Tony Brown, the secretary at Somerset CCC between 1982 and 1988, arriving at the County Ground near the start of his time in office.

'Retain Viv, Joel, Ian' – four staunch supporters of the Big Three, including Marcia Hayes (right) and Jane White (second from left in front of husband Peter) let their feelings be known.

Ian Botham turning up at the County Ground for one of the last times before his departure.

A group of the Big Three supporters show their feelings at the County Ground.

Standing room only for the national media in front of the Press Box during a big one day game at the County Ground.

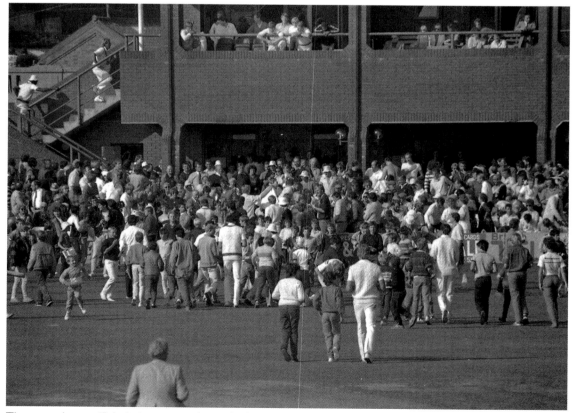

The crowds engulf their heroes at the end of another one day game at the County Ground.

Somerset fans rally to support the Big Three in 1986.

Ian Botham's mother pictured among the crowd at the County Ground below the steps to the home dressing room in front of the Colin Atkinson Pavilion.

Ian Botham pictured on the visitors' balcony with his father Les on his first return to play at the County Ground for Worcestershire in 1987. Steven Rhodes the Worcestershire keeper is left of the picture.

Somerset v West Indies XI. The visitors opening batsmen make their way to the wicket in front of a packed County Ground.

Joel Garner in full flight action at the Taunton ground.

Peter Robinson, coaching a group of young cricketers in the old Indoor School.

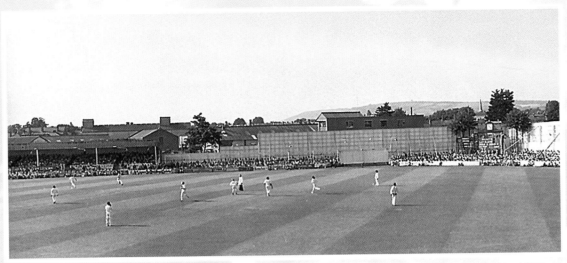

Somerset in action at the County Ground before the opening of the Colin Atkinson Pavilion in 1979, which now stands in the corner occupied by the old main scoreboard.

'In memory of Three Great Cricketers'. A wreath was laid at the County Ground after the departure of Ian Botham, Joel Garner and Viv Richards.

Somerset coach
Peter Robinson
suitably attired
in my Russian
Cossack hat,
batting snow
balls at the
County Ground
with Dennis
Breakwell
standing in wait
for the icy catch.

Above and overleaf: The Somerset crowd gathers in front of the Colin Atkinson Pavilion at the end of a Sunday League game.

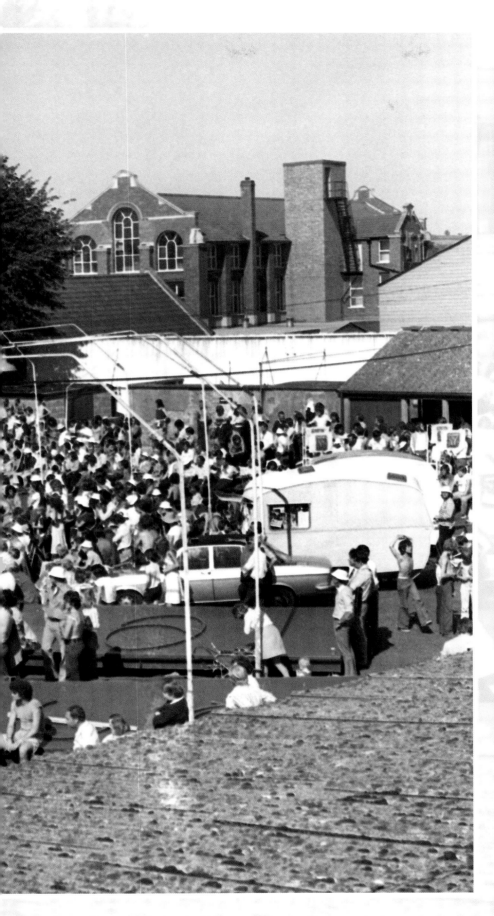

The view of the County Ground on a busy one day match taken from the roof of the old Indoor School. Note the lime trees in front of Barnicott's Building, the overhead lights around the boundary edge that were used when the ground hosted greyhound racing and the deck chairs around the boundary edge.

Viv Richards is given a hero's welcome as he leaves the field at the County Ground after another scintillating innings during the early part of his career.

The heavy roller being brought out to roll the wicket at the County Ground.

The Executive Business Club at the County Ground that stood for many years next door to the Stragglers Bar on the Brewhouse Theatre side of the ground.

Somerset always attracted huge crowds for their home matches in the one day competitions during the Glory Years. The temporary stand, which has been erected in front of the 'cowshed' stand is packed to the rafters.

The JCR bus that served as the club shop for a number of years is seen here parked on the Barnicott's side of the County Ground.

A groundsman at work at the County Ground.

Single wicket
competition – a
young Alain Lockyer!
Photo courtesy of
Mike Williams

England captain Bob
Willis taking a
photograph of me
taking delivery of a
car.

Dry Blackthorn Trophy and Other Presentations

Viv Richards and his namesake Barry Richards – arguably two of the greatest batsmen of their time, pictured together ahead of taking part in the Taunton Cider Dry Blackthorn Trophy challenge at the County Ground which was a very popular annual event at that time.

Viv and Barry Richards pictured at the County Ground ahead of another Taunton Cider Dry Blackthorn Trophy duel! The man in the middle is Roger Wotton who acted as the second.

Miles Roberts the MD of Taunton Cider making a presentation to Viv Richards in the early days of the Dry Blackthorn Challenge Trophy at the County Ground.

Barry Richards pictured with Miles Roberts on the same occasion.

A young Ian Botham after receiving a presentation from Len Creed, who was responsible for bringing Viv Richards to Somerset and was the Chairman of SCCC 1977-78.

Vic Marks receives an award on the balcony of the Colin Atkinson Pavilion. Also pictured is Michael Hill who was the Chairman of SCCC at that time.

Ian Botham relaxing during the batting period of the game.

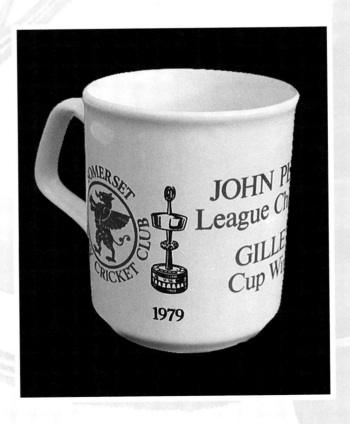

Somerset CCC produced a special Double Winners Mug in 1979 to celebrate their double one day success in the Gillette Cup and John Player League.

William Rees Mogg, the editor of *The Times*, making a presentation to Joel Garner. Also in the picture are Graham Burgess (second from left) and Peter Denning (second from the right).

Miles Roberts the Chairman of Taunton Cider makes a presentation to Somerset captain Brian Rose at the end of another Dry Blackthorn Trophy match.

Len Creed, the Chairman of Somerset 1977-78, making a presentation to Brian Close who captained the County between 1972 and '77.

Brian Close was already 40 years old when he joined Somerset from his native Yorkshire but under his stewardship the Glory Years team developed. This is another early picture of mine.

Viv Richards being presented with the Dry
Blackthorn Trophy by the Chairman of Taunton
Cider, Miles Roberts.

Viv Richards tries out a new healthy drink!

Lord's Finals and Somerset Celebrations

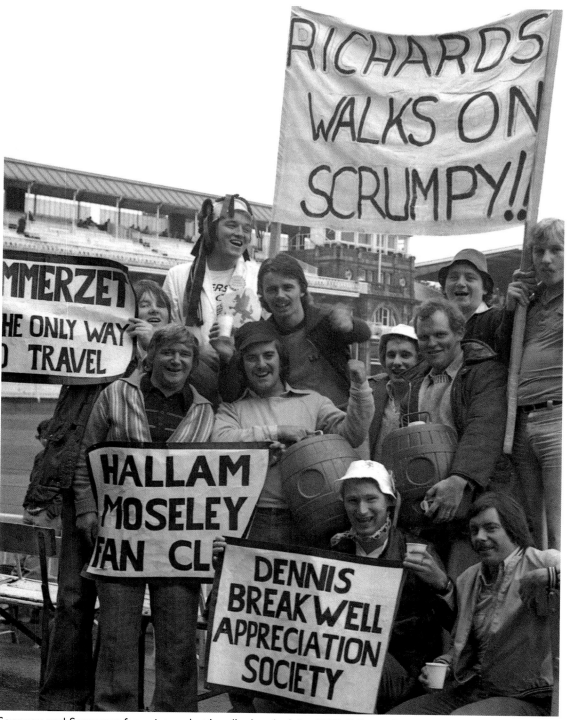

Scrumpy and Somerset fans pictured at Lord's ahead of the 1979 Gillette Cup Final, where they beat Northamptonshire – their first ever trophy. The previous year they had been denied by Sussex at Lord's.

Somerset fans flock onto the pitch at Lord's to catch a glimpse of their heroes after the history-making victory over Northamptonshire in the Gillette Cup Final in September 1979.

Somerset captain Brian Rose holds the Gillette Cup aloft at Lord's in September 1979, the county's first ever taste of glory.

Somerset fans take a break between the innings in the B and H Final 1981.

Zumerset Zider Boys! The Somerset fans always added colour to all of the Cup Final matches that they played at Lord's. Another scene from the 1981 B and H Final.

It has been a long hot day at Lord's after a very early start. Somerset fans take a well earned rest between the innings during a one day final.

Somerset fans have some more silverware to celebrate as they invade the pitch after another one day success at Lord's. It seems as though even the Wombles were supporting Somerset on this occasion!

Big Bird eats Rice for Breakfast. Somerset fans back their favourite bowler Joel Garner to get the better of Nottinghamshire's Clive Rice at Lord's in 1982, where the County triumphed comfortably by 9 wickets.

Somerset fans show their appreciation for the team after they have just beaten Nottinghamshire in the Benson and Hedges Cup Final in 1982.

This group of Somerset supporters look quietly confident that their team will win the Benson and Hedges Final at Lord's in 1982.

Somerset fans celebrate the B and H victory at Lord's in 1982.

Time for a rest
between the
innings at Lord's
in 1982.

More Somerset
fans at Lord's in
1982.

The Long and the Short of it! A Somerset fan has to improvise to get on level terms to talk with Joel Garner ahead of the Benson and Hedges Final at Lord's.

Viv Richards is 'Singing in the Rain' outside the Grace Gates at Lord's ahead of the 1981 Benson and Hedges Cup Final.

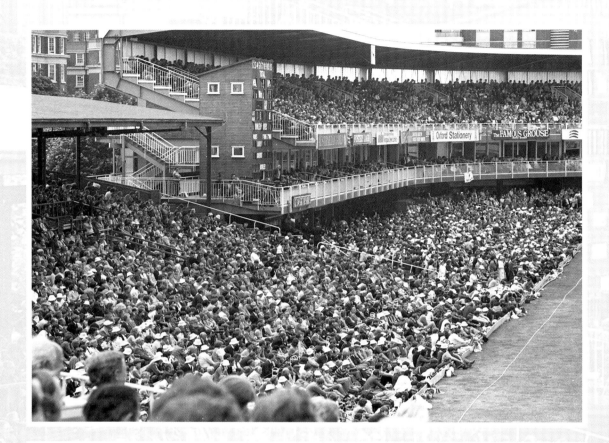

Lord's Cricket Ground was always full to bursting when Somerset appeared in any one day cup final.

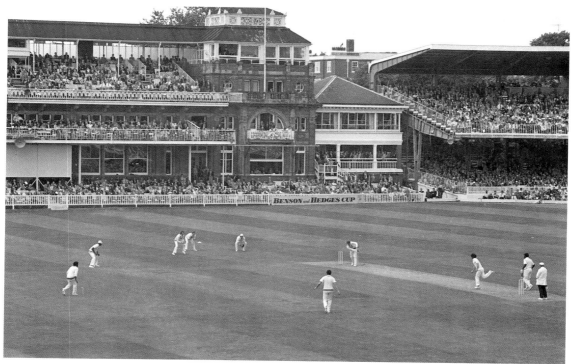

Somerset in action in front of a packed house at Lord's on Benson and Hedges Cup Final Day.

Somerset fans celebrate another one day victory at Lord's Cricket Ground.

The Somerset balcony is a happy place to be as they look down on their team collecting the trophy and winners' medals at Lord's.

Included among those on the balcony are Trevor Gard, far left, Dennis Waight, Sunil Gavaskar, Gary Palmer back left, Peter Robinson in blazer, front left, President Colin Atkinson front in white jacket, Max Jeffrey front in suit, Keith Jennings behind him Nigel Felton and Hallam Moseley.

At one of the Lord's Cup Finals camera manufacturers Maniya gave me the new 500mm lens to use on a 6x7 camera. This was the first time for a revolutionary lens.

Somerset crowds enjoy another big day out at Lord's.

Cricket at Weston-super-Mare

Peter Roebuck walking back to the pavilion at Weston-super-Mare after being dismissed against Worcestershire.

Vic Marks looks hopefully at the umpire after an appeal against him by the Worcestershire bowlers at Weston-super-Mare.

Peter Roebuck.

Snooker player Jimmy White and guest get the VIP treatment at Clarence Park in Weston-super-Mare.

Clarence Park at Weston-super-Mare on a busy match day.

Jesmond Floodlit Game Northumberland v Somerset

Action from one of the very early floodlit games in England, that was hosted at Jesmond and sponsored by Taunton Cider. Somerset played against Northumberland.

The Somerset team arriving at Newcastle Airport ahead of a floodlit game at Jesmond against Northumberland, that was sponsored by Taunton Cider.

The team flew from Bristol in two small aircraft, a journey that some members of the team did not enjoy. While the players were fortunate to have flown to the north east I had to drive myself to the match.

Pictured right to left are Peter Roebuck, Brian Rose, Vic Marks, Viv Richards, Joel Garner, Ian Botham, Peter Denning, Jock McCombe, Jeremy Lloyds, Phil Slocombe, Colin Dredge (partly hidden), Nigel Felton and Trevor Gard.

'The King and I' – Viv Richards and Ian Botham arriving at Newcastle Airport en route to the floodlit limited overs match at Jesmond Cricket Club between Northumberland and Somerset CCC.

Signing autographs for some young fans after being dismissed at the Jesmond floodlit game.

Ian Botham: Charity Walks and Rides

Ian Botham pictured with his assistant Andy Withers ahead of his charity fund raising Hannibal's Walk over the Alps. The Hannibal's Walk took place after Ian's first fund raising trek from John O'Groats to Land's End for Leukaemia Research in 1985 and was for the same charity.

Ian Botham on one of his Leukaemia charity walks accompanied by England captain Mike Gatting.

Ian Botham and Mike Gatting pictured together later in the day on the same charity walk.

Ian Botham preparing for his charity Hannibal's Walk.

Ian Botham passing through West Huntspill on one of his fund raising charity walks. Also in the picture are Michael Hill, the Chairman of SCCC (right of ITB, wearing cap) boxer John Conteh (immediately right of ITB) and sports presenter Dickie Davies (immediately left).

Ian Botham: Dedicated Follower of Fashion

Ian Botham – dedicated follower of fashion pictured at the back of the Castle Hotel in Taunton. Ian linked up with Tim Hudson to develop his own brand of clothing.

Modelling for Tim Hudson in the grounds of the Castle Hotel at Taunton.

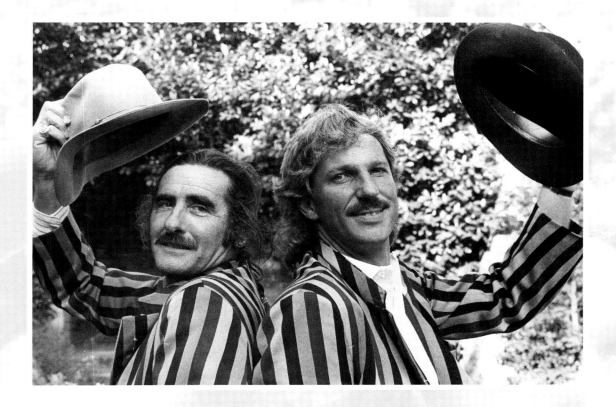

Tim Hudson (left) and Ian Botham model their new range of clothing in the gardens of the Castle Hotel.

Ian Botham in front of the Castle Hotel in Taunton.

Castle Hotel Meeting

In 1986 Somerset CCC decided not to renew the contracts of Garner and Richards and this precipitated the departure of Botham. An outcry from some members led to a meeting at the Castle Hotel, when the arguments for and against were put to the committee. The committee decided to call an SGM which was held at the Royal Bath and West Showground, Shepton Mallet on 8 November. Although tensions ran high, the original decision was upheld and the departure of the Big Three was confirmed.

Top table at the Castle Hotel meeting, left to Bridget Langdon, Peter White, Richard Weston and Michael Gould.

Bridget Langdon and Peter Roebuck pictured together at the meeting at the Castle Hotel in Taunton.

Richard Weston and Michael Gould pictured at the Castle Hotel in Taunton.

Shepton Mallet Meeting

Members gathering at the Bath and West Showground at Shepton Mallet ahead of the special general meeting on Saturday 8 November 1986.

Peter Roebuck, the Captain of SCCC at the Shepton Mallet meeting.

Joel Garner arriving at the Shepton Mallet meeting.

Nigel Popplewell arriving at the Shepton Mallet meeting.

Marie and Les Botham queuing to get into the Shepton Mallet meeting.

Graham Burgess, who retired after winning the double in 1979, pictured ahead of the Shepton Mallet meeting.

Top table at the Bath and West Showground meeting at Shepton Mallet. Left to right Brian Langford, Peter Roebuck, Michael Hill, Richard Weston, Bridget Langdon and Peter White.

Colin Atkinson (right), the President of SCCC and Michael Hill the Chairman at the meeting at Shepton Mallet.

The 'Big Three' Return to Somerset
Glory Years Recaptured

Viv Richards returned to the County Ground to be awarded his honorary life membership of Somerset CCC in 1994.

Viv Richards back at the County Ground. The official opening of the Sir Vivian Richards Gates preceded the great man's final innings at the County Ground when he played for Lashings CC against Somerset when he eased his way to 16, including two fours and a mighty six, much to the delight of the large and appreciative crowd who were present.

This page and overleaf: In 2008 Ian Botham began his 12th Charity Walk for Leukaemia Research at the County Ground.

Somerset bowling legend Joel Garner returned to the County Ground to be presented with his Honorary Life Membership of Somerset CCC in 2009.

On the same visit Joel Garner opened the new gates that were named in his honour, accompanied by his daughter Jewel.